ORWELL IN AMERICA

Joe Sutton

I0139058

BROADWAY PLAY PUBLISHING INC
224 E 62nd St, NY, NY 10065
www.broadwayplaypub.com
info@broadwayplaypub.com

ORWELL IN AMERICA
© Copyright 2017 Joe Sutton

Cover artwork by Alan Buttar, www.musedesign.co.uk

First edition: July 2017
I S B N: 978-0-88145-707-0

Book design: Marie Donovan
Page make-up: Adobe InDesign
Typeface: Palatino
Printed and bound in the U S A

To my beautiful wife Anne

The World Premiere of ORWELL IN AMERICA
was produced by Northern Stage (Carol Dunne,
Artistic Director; Eric Bunge, Managing Director) in
White River Junction, Vermont. The opening night
performance took place on 14 March 2015 with the
following cast and creative contributors:

GEORGE ORWELL .... Jamie Horton
CARLOTTA .... Allison Jean White
DELIVERY BOY .... Trevor Siegel

Director .... Peter Hackett
Production stage manager .... Danielle Zandri
Assistant stage manager .... Colleen Lacy
Scenic designer .... Caite Hevner
Costume designer .... Amy Sutton
Lighting designer .... Stuart Duke
Sound designer .... Ben Montmagny

The New York Premiere of ORWELL IN AMERICA
was presented by 59e59 Theaters: (Elysabeth
Kleinhans, President & Artistic Director; Peter Tear,
Executive Producer) and produced by Northern Stage.
The cast and creative contributors were:

GEORGE ORWELL ....Jamie Horton
CARLOTTA ....Jeanna De Waal
YOUNG MAN... Casey Predovic

Director...Peter Hackett
Production stage manager ....Whitney Keeter
Assistant stage manager....................................Lela Gannon
Scenic designer... Caite Hevner
Costume designer.. Amy Sutton
Lighting designer... Stuart Duke
Sound designer.. Ben Montmagny

CHARACTERS & SETTING

GEORGE ORWELL, *tall, lean, and seeming quite old—though only 45*

CARLOTTA MORRISON, *also tall, and very beautiful, late 20s*

There is also a "Young Man" —as well as a variety of "Voices" that are heard throughout.

Time: Just after World War Two

Place: Small town America

Setting: The play moves back and forth, sometimes very rapidly, between two areas: an auditorium stage and a hotel room. These settings represent the many such hotel rooms and auditorium stages that GEORGE ORWELL *will visit in his month-long tour of North America. For our purposes, it is important to realize that these transitions can happen in the blink of an eye. What starts in the hotel room can sometimes, mid-sentence, transition to an enormous, public auditorium, and then, in the very next sentence, transfer back to the hotel room. It's like a jump cut in film. We move back and forth in a flash.*

Text: Please note that a dash at the end of a line (—) means the speaker is interrupted; where an ellipsis (…) indicates that the speaker has trailed off.

ACT ONE

(The lights come up on a self-conscious man with an odd little smile. In truth he's a bit shy, but you can't really tell it because he speaks so aggressively.)

ORWELL: My name is Eric Blair.
(And his voice is rather plummy-sounding.)
Now I know you've all come to see George Orwell…
(The man he actually is.)
…but I'm afraid you'll have to make do with Eric Blair.
(He seems rather pleased with himself.)

CARLOTTA: That's it. Come downstage.
(This last comes from a woman sitting off the to side—in shadows.)

ORWELL: Now of course… *(Abruptly, frustrated)* …oh, what is it?
(He's forgotten his speech.)

CARLOTTA: *(Jumping in)* That's it. You're doing fine.

(But quickly ORWELL remembers it.)

ORWELL: This is the point where I could say that Mister Orwell will be with you next month. Or that he's next door. Or that the Kiwanis Club will be sponsoring a dinner on his behalf after the first of the year! But instead I'll say that I am Orwell too. That is I, *also*, am Orwell. Not that there are two Orwells. There is only one, and I am he!

(This last ORWELL *says irate, furious at himself for over-complicating.* CARLOTTA *interjects.)*

CARLOTTA: You may want to simplify that.

ORWELL: *(Overlapping)* Which raises the question, "well then, *who*…is this Mister Blair?" And the only answer is Mister Blair was Mister Orwell before Mister Orwell became himself.

CARLOTTA: I—

ORWELL: *(Loudly)* May I continue? Please?!? Really…I…appreciate your…but please, *do* let me continue.
(He returns to his audience—his "imaginary" audience.)
That is Mister Orwell…
(Aside) you may want to write down your notes in pencil… *(Resuming)* …Mister Orwell, the name Mister Blair is now commonly *known by*, is what we call a "nom de plume". It is not his, that is *my real* name. My real name, the name my parents gave me, the name I took to Saint Cyprian School and then on to the fields of *Eton*…was Blair.

CARLOTTA: Good.

ORWELL: It was Blair when I went to Burma as well. I…
(Then, suddenly, blowing up) …No, I'm sorry. I can't do this!

(The lights come up on a hotel room.)

CARLOTTA: Can't do what?

(As ORWELL *turns around on a truly spectacular-looking woman sitting across from him. The scene is actually taking place just moments after she's arrived. He's been rehearsing.)*

ORWELL: Practice! I'm much too distracted!

CARLOTTA: By what?

ORWELL: You!

CARLOTTA: In what sense?

ORWELL: You're too beautiful.

CARLOTTA: Oh—now—

ORWELL: Oh, don't tell me you don't know it! You know it!

CARLOTTA: Look—

ORWELL: Beside the fact—you're not what I expected. *(He stomps over to a side table—petulantly.)*

CARLOTTA: How so?

ORWELL: You signed your name Carlton. You said your name was Carlton!

CARLOTTA: I did, yes.

ORWELL: Why?!?

(ORWELL's back is to CARLOTTA.)

CARLOTTA: Because I was afraid you wouldn't see me if I signed my name Carlotta. Would you have?

ORWELL: Yes, I think so. *(Beat, less certain)* I think I would have, yes.

CARLOTTA: Well, I couldn't be sure, and so I signed my letter Carlton. *(Pause)* Please forgive me.

(ORWELL watches CARLOTTA a moment—then suddenly blurts out.)

ORWELL: I need a new wife.

CARLOTTA: Pardon me?

ORWELL: My first wife is dead. I'm in need of another.

CARLOTTA: Yes, well you're also in need of a publicist.

ORWELL: Would you consider it?

CARLOTTA: Being your publicist?

ORWELL: Being my wife!

CARLOTTA: No. Mister Orwell.

ORWELL: Mister Blair!

CARLOTTA: Mister Blair. No. (*Long pause*) But thank you for the offer.

(ORWELL *unscrews a whiskey bottle.* CARLOTTA *watches him. She is now the one who's annoyed.*)

CARLOTTA: Mister Orwell.

ORWELL: Blair.

CARLOTTA: Perhaps you should—

ORWELL: (*Short*) You've declined the wifely role. Have you not?

CARLOTTA: I have.

ORWELL: Very well then.
(*He now returns with his drink.*)
Now then. You were saying.

CARLOTTA: (*Unsure*) Up to you—I should think.

ORWELL: Where were we?

CARLOTTA: Burma.

ORWELL: Burma, yes. Burm— Actually this brings up an interesting thought. Whether I should detail the various thoughts I was having, the various "events" of my life—the travel, the fighting, Spain…Morocco… (*Somewhat pointed*) …my wife—whether I should *detail* all that…

CARLOTTA: Absolutely!

ORWELL: Or whether I should start by saying the following…

CARLOTTA: Oh, for—

ORWELL: I am a man of the Left.

(CARLOTTA's *pencil breaks.*)

CARLOTTA: That—

ORWELL: Whatever else you may think you have heard… *(A beat)* …whatever else you may *know*…know that first and foremost. I am a man of the Left. I believe in Socialism.

CARLOTTA: You can't say that.

(CARLOTTA and ORWELL are in the hotel again.)

ORWELL: Why not?

CARLOTTA: You… *(Fed up)* Mister Orwell, be serious!

ORWELL: I *am* being serious! It's the whole point!

CARLOTTA: It is not the whole point.

ORWELL: It is!

CARLOTTA: You can't tell an American audience you're a *socialist!*

ORWELL: Why not?

CARLOTTA: Because of the moment we're in, that's why! Because…Mister Orwell, could I just say two words to you? *Two words!* Before you go on? *Animal Farm!!!!*
(She cries these words out!)
That's what the people want to hear. That's… People want to hear you talk about Communism, for God's sake. The red menace. And look, I'm not saying these other topics aren't interesting. They are. But this is a book tour! And on a book tour you must *talk about your book!* The…here…let… "People sleep peaceably at night"… Yes? Do you remember this?
(She has retrieved a batch of index cards which she now reads from.)
"People sleep peaceably at night because *rough* men stand ready to do *violence* on their behalf."
(Another card)

"To survive it is often necessary to *fight*. And to fight
you must *dirty* yourself."

ORWELL: *(Smiling, quietly)* You've done your research.

CARLOTTA: "War is *evil*, but it is often the *lesser*...of
evils." *Those* are ideas that people want to hear. Not...
And again, I'm not saying these other ideas aren't
interesting. They are. But you must give the people
what they want! You—

ORWELL: *(Cutting her off)* I will, Miss Morrison. *(Beat)* I
assure you. I will.

(CARLOTTA stares daggers at ORWELL.)

ORWELL: But I don't think—and please, before you take
issue, consider: I don't think it's best to go straight *at it*.
I think it's best to go the way round. To... And look, I
may be very wrong about this, but I think some of our
audience may be very *happy*...to hear what I have to
say about language—for instance. After all, these are
literary clubs, aren't they? They're not "beer halls". Are
they?

CARLOTTA: *(Grudging)* No.

ORWELL: So...let's not sell them short, shall we? Let's...
(He winks.) ...let's see what they can reach.

*(At this point the lights suddenly come up on an auditorium,
a "1940's" auditorium...)*

ORWELL: Now then, why is it *important*??
*(Where he, having practiced his speech, is now truly a
"showman".)*
And again, thank you so much for coming here tonight.
For being our first audience. I'm just thrilled with
this! But yes, why must we care about the language
we use; the subject we're on. I mean, good God, what
difference does it make—if we use a German word
instead of an English. Because our thinking blurs...
that's why. Because...

CARLOTTA: *(In half light, to herself)* Not bad.

(ORWELL *glances over as he speaks.)*

ORWELL: …when we speak in such a way, we cease to fully *experience* what we are saying. When we adopt these shortcuts—and this goes for pet phrases as well— "the nub of it", "shoe on the other foot", "throw down the gauntlet" when we stop thinking about what we are saying and instead reach for the ready-made phrase…a reaction occurs we did not anticipate. We begin to allow our *words* to do our *thinking* for us. And that way well…that way lies madness, doesn't it? That way—and correct me if I'm wrong—but that way the inmates are running the asylum, aren't they? In a way? *(With a twinkle)* As it were?
(Again he glance over at CARLOTTA, *his eyebrows raised.)*

ORWELL: Do you see? A joke.

CARLOTTA: *(Amused)* I…yes…

ORWELL: You're not laughing.

CARLOTTA: I'm…inside I am.

ORWELL: *(Continuing, without pause)* In any case, Blair, Orwell, *who is he?* Well, it happens I did in fact live in France. Just after Burma and coming home and deciding to be a writer, I thought, hey now, the best way to do that is to go to France. Why I thought such a thing, I have no idea. After all, it isn't as if the poor aren't in England. And that's what I was writing about at the time. The poor. In fact, I later went on to write an entire book about the miners in the north. *The Road to Wigan Pier.* But for some reason at the very start there, it was France. I *had* to get to France.

CARLOTTA: Actually—

ORWELL: Actually, speaking of France has anyone got a cigarette? I seem…
(He pats down his pockets.)

Oh, no, hang on. I have one.
(Removing a pack)
Actually, more than one. Do...
(He laughs.)
...actually this brings up an idea...
(He takes out a cigarette, lighting it.)
...speaking of France, the poor, the life I was leading at
that time...there is nothing that better *defines* that life
than the relations I had with my cigarettes.
(Taking a puff)
That everyone had actually. All around. With mere
pennies in our pockets, shillings, a few francs, we
would have to decide which came first...food, wine...
or tobacco.

CARLOTTA: *(Grudging, unhappy)* Again, not bad—

ORWELL: *(Aside)* I just needed some encouragement.

CARLOTTA: *(Frustrated)* But it's not a title we've come
for, Mister Orwell! The...*The Road to Wigan Pier* is not a
title we recognize!

(Again the lights are on the hotel, and CARLOTTA *is
suddenly quite angry.)*

CARLOTTA: And if you'd done a book tour at *that* time,
and forgive me for speaking so bluntly, but if you'd
done a book tour at that time, there would have been
no audience for you. Now there is! I mean, good God,
you've sold three hundred thousand books here!
That's—

ORWELL: Mister Blair.

CARLOTTA: *(Annoyed)* Pardon me?

ORWELL: You said Orwell again. It's Blair.

CARLOTTA: That—

ORWELL: Although I wouldn't mind Eric.

CARLOTTA: That is an incredible accomplishment, Mister...Blair. But you've got to talk about your book. You've got to talk about *Animal Farm*!!!

ORWELL: I will, Miss Morrison! As I told you...I will! But...good God...it's not entirely about the damn book! It...I have something I would like to *add* to it!

CARLOTTA: *(Angrily)* About socialism?

ORWELL: About many things! But yes, right, about socialism.

(CARLOTTA shakes her head, truly impatient with ORWELL.)

CARLOTTA: Well...I mean, really, this is what they're afraid of. This... *(Beat)* Oh, never mind.

ORWELL: What were you going to say?

CARLOTTA: Nothing. I—

ORWELL: No, you were going to say something. What— and *who*? Miss Morrison. You say "they" were afraid. Who is "they"?

CARLOTTA: Who do you think, Mister Blair? My goodness. Your publishers. My employers! Be reasonable!

ORWELL: In what sense am I *not* being reasonable?

CARLOTTA: In the sense that you are not recalling the exchanges you had before you got here! That's how! This is a very difficult moment we're having in America. Surely you're aware of that. And your publisher, my company is concerned with it. Surely you can't be surprised by that.

ORWELL: I am not. In fact, it is the reason I agreed-- and you can see, of course, how happy I am that I did—to *accept* your company. *(He is being sarcastic.)* What I did not do was agree to—and I would appreciate your not suggesting I did—was being muzzled! And besides, and this is what I truly *don't* understand, what on

earth are you objecting to? At this point, we're talking
about romance. Aren't we? About a young man. His
cigarettes. How—
(Turning back to the audience. Exaggerated)
And a horror in such moments
(Only to briefly glance back at her.)
And believe me, our audiences, in Chicago, Akron,
wherever we are, our audiences will appreciate it. I
guarantee you.
*(Again to the audience—about to joke about tobacco
"shortages")*
The horror in such moments—

CARLOTTA: Still—I just—

ORWELL: Oh, for god's *sake!*

CARLOTTA: I just—

ORWELL: Would you PLEASE!

(CARLOTTA and ORWELL are again in the hotel.)

CARLOTTA: I must—

ORWELL: No, you must *not*. I must insist. You must not!

CARLOTTA: That's—

ORWELL: Don't—

CARLOTTA: Mister Blair, I must *correct* you!
(She is furious; her words tumbling out)
You seem to be under the mistaken impression that
I am somehow here because I am low man on the
totem pole at my publishing firm! Or because I have
a habit of making a positive impression on middle-
aged men when I am wearing a sweater. Or because,
although it's true, I am a distant relation of Mister
Ernest Hemingway's! That is *not* why I'm here! I am
here for a number of reasons, chief among these the
fact that I graduated top of my class, from a prestigious
collage, with a double degree in comparative literature

and politics! I am also here because I was the most enthusiastic of everyone asked about *taking* this assignment! Those are the reasons I am here. And I would appreciate you keeping them in mind.

ORWELL: Which...prestigious college?

CARLOTTA: Pardon me???

ORWELL: Which—

CARLOTTA: Vassar.

ORWELL: Never heard of it.

CARLOTTA: *(Spitting out)* It will do, Mister Orwell. It will do.

(ORWELL steps back, truly struck by CARLOTTA.)

ORWELL: As will you, my dear. As will you.

CARLOTTA: Now then—

ORWELL: However...before we go on...can we not have an agreement? I promise you, I will listen to everything you have to say. All of it. Every word. But can I ask that you please let me finish what I have to say before you begin?

CARLOTTA: I—

ORWELL: Please. Can we not agree to that?

(ORWELL holds out his hand for CARLOTTA to shake.)

CARLOTTA: Very well. We... *(Beat)* Yes.

(CARLOTTA and ORWELL shake. He smiles.)

ORWELL: Mister Ernest Hemingway, huh?

CARLOTTA: Hemingway, yes. A distant... My... *(Waving her hand)* ...I don't even know who.

ORWELL: A fact you didn't overstress in your job interview, I shouldn't think.

CARLOTTA: No.

ORWELL: No.

(ORWELL looks at her, growing ever more charmed.)

ORWELL: Very well then. Where were we?

CARLOTTA: France.

ORWELL: France, yes. I—

CARLOTTA: Oh. One minute.

ORWELL: Pardon me?

CARLOTTA: I…have another thought.

ORWELL: Oh?

(CARLOTTA looks at ORWELL, realizing he is becoming irked.)

CARLOTTA: Actually no. I'm sorry. Go ahead. Please. Continue.

(And now it is ORWELL who looks at CARLOTTA. Stares at her really.)

ORWELL: Tell me something. What do you think of me?

CARLOTTA: In what sense?

ORWELL: As I stand before you. *(Beat)* As a man. What do you think?

CARLOTTA: I'm… *(Searching)* …impressed.

ORWELL: By my appearance? By my mind? In what way?

CARLOTTA: By your work.

(This last catches ORWELL off guard. He hadn't expected it.)

ORWELL: Oh? You know my work?

CARLOTTA: Well, of course I know your work. I… *(Laughing, stating the obvious)* Yes!

(Brief pause)

ORWELL: And which do you like best? Of all of my books? If you had to say now?

CARLOTTA: Well, I like each one of them. Each in its own way. *(Beat)* But really, Mister… *(About to say "Orwell" she corrects herself)* …Blair…let's I shouldn't have interrupted. Please. Continue.

ORWELL: Please tell me.
(His voice suddenly seems needy. Raw. Vulnerable.)

ORWELL: Of all of my books. *(Beat)* Not counting *Animal Farm.* Which do you like best?

(And CARLOTTA realizes in that instant just how vulnerable ORWELL is. And how much he needs her to answer. And she wants to. But before she does, she takes a moment.)

CARLOTTA: If I had to say now? *(Slight beat) Down and out in Paris and London. (Slight pause)* Because of what you just said. I just…love it.

ORWELL: You do?

CARLOTTA: I do…yes. I…

(ORWELL is moved by CARLOTTA's earnestness.)

CARLOTTA: You have a wonderful eye…Mister… *(Beat, heartfelt)* Wonderful.

(And for a moment ORWELL is silent. Then, embarrassed perhaps, he decides to move on.)

ORWELL: Well, if I had, I soon lost it. Or misplaced it, I guess I should say. I mean, good God, those next three books? Absolute nonsense, no? Total— *(Getting wound up)* I mean, I think back on those books even now… *(Again he turns to the audience—the "entertainer".)* …and wonder how on *earth*… You see, there was in many of the books I was writing in those days, those three in particular, an absolute *desperation*…in my writing. So desperate was I to be a writer, so consumed…was I by the fear that I would never write again, that I wrote about whatever was occurring. No matter how dull, how...uninteresting. It didn't— *(Quickly changing)* Of course there was another desperation that marched briskly alongside. That I would never find a wife. That... Actually, that wasn't really it. That I would never find sex! That was *truly* what was on my mind. And I thought about it day and night. More than I thought about Hitler even! *(Beat)* And I needn't tell you that I was thinking about Hitler a good deal in those days.

CARLOTTA: Mister—

ORWELL: But really, in those days, women were number one. And here's where I got truly lucky. Really...astonishingly so. For after a few years of utter privation...and many instances much too embarrassing to recount I met Eileen O'Shaunessy. The woman who would...almost instantly...
(His voice catching when he says this)
...become my wife.
(Then, because it does *catch, he moves on, embarrassed.)*
And then, man that I was, in order that she not get the wrong idea about me, I left for Spain. Truly. Within a matter of weeks. Off!
(Then, he's on a roll.)
At this point, you must understand that Spain was literally the *center* of our universe. At this point, it seemed more than possible that a Republic—smack dab in the center of Europe—could, if things went badly, go *under. Or...* *(Half-turning, quick)* ...Actually, I should say a word here about Spain. It wasn't *truly* what we were after. What we were *truly* after was Europe. The Continent. Spain was merely the test case. If Hitler and Mussolini could overthrow a Republic in Spain, why then they could overthrow Republics everywhere. They could overthrow everything. The could rule the entire *world!* And we were determined

that that would not happen. And so it was that men from all over that world came together and determined that we would *safeguard* that Republic, and march—arm in arm—into the future!

VOICE: Into a Communist future!

(This last surprises ORWELL. *He hadn't expected it.)*

ORWELL: Excuse me?

VOICE: What you're talking about—that was Communism!

(At this, the lights come up on CARLOTTA—*even as they remain up on* ORWELL *in the auditorium as well.)*

CARLOTTA: You see, this is what I was afraid of. Peop... *(New idea)* That—

ORWELL: *(Outraged, to the man)* May I continue, please?

VOICE: I'm just saying.

ORWELL: I understand that. *But may I continue???* *(He waits to see if the man will let him continue. He is again furious.)*

ORWELL: Thank you. *(Then, not backing down)* I will take up what you've said... *(Beat)* ...but first let me continue with what *I* was saying. *(Again he waits. Then, just as he's about to resume, he instead rushes over to the man, confronting him directly.)* It was *not* Communism. The point I'm making is it was *not* Communism. In fact, I soon went to King Street, Communist Party headquarters and told them that I would *not* join their International Brigade!

(The lights return to the hotel, CARLOTTA *beside herself!)*

CARLOTTA: Which the man did not *understand.* To him Spain *is* Communism. It *is* the International Brigade. And so for you to suggest that you didn't join them, but that you *did* go to Spain...that's just not a distinction he's going to be able to make. *(Practically*

frothing) People at that part of the talk wanted you to
say what you'd come to say. What they *thought* you'd
come to say. Which is that Communism, whether it's
King Street, whether it's Stalin, cannot be romanticized.
That it's *evil*. That our worry about poverty, about
"miners", as you so often wrote about, all too often
forces us to embrace *evil*. Without understanding that
that is what we're doing! Yes, of course, the animals on
Animal Farm have been mistreated, but the solution...
as you so eloquently tell us...is not collectivist. It's not
clear what the solution is...but it is *not* collectivist!

ORWELL: No! The solution is not "party"! The solution
is not "hierarchy"! The solution is not allowing
"glorious ends" to blind us from necessarily despicable
means! But that is not socialism, Miss Morrison. That
is...Communism! That is...I mean, for God's sake,
do you not understand the moment we're in?? Our
country at the moment in history is *suffering*?? England
is suffering! The *world*, beneath the equator, as it *always*
does, is suffering! And we must do something—Good
God Almighty!—we must do something to *alleviate*
that suffering. And we cannot allow Stalin...this is
the entire point of my talk...we cannot allow Stalin, a
Com-mu-nist... *(Emphasizing each syllable)* ...to tarnish
the good name of *socialism* and *keep us* from alleviating
that "suffering"!!! *(Having raised his voice—he now
pauses.)* I will not...I am sorry that you don't approve
of it...but I will *not* change my message. That is what
I've come to say. That—

CARLOTTA: May I say one other thing...in that case? On
an entirely different subject?

*(ORWELL, upset, nods his head. And CARLOTTA, equally
upset, continues.)*

CARLOTTA: Your drinking.

ORWELL: *(Snapping)* What about it?

CARLOTTA: You're not...how to say it...you're not putting yourself in your best light.

ORWELL: Oh? Do tell. What "light" am I putting myself in?

CARLOTTA: Perhaps you would consider...
(Barely controlled) ...waiting until *after* your talk before you "begin your evening".

ORWELL: You know Miss Morrison, I'm not sure if you've noticed...but I haven't exactly enjoyed this first week of ours. It hasn't come easily to me. And so I'm afraid I'm going to have to continue with what you so clearly consider my "distasteful" practice. However... and perhaps this will assuage...I am more than happy to "share" what I've managed to garner...with such a "concerned" colleague.

CARLOTTA: No...I... *(Beat)* Thank you.

ORWELL: You don't partake?

CARLOTTA: I... *(About to offer a fuller explanation, she instead cuts herself off)* No.

ORWELL: Pity. *(Beat)* But so marvelous that you've reminded me. *(With this, he goes to a bottle and pours.)* Now then.

CARLOTTA: We don't—we don't have to practice any more.

ORWELL: *(Sarcastic)* Oh, please. I'm enjoying it. Really.

CARLOTTA: We—

ORWELL: No, really—where were we? Ah, yes, King Street. British Communism. So yes, I did ask for their help and at the same time turned up my nose at their Legion. Which meant, predictably, that they turned me down.
(And again he is in front of the audience, the "showman". And again, he's energetic!)

...Which in turn meant that I had to find another way of getting there. For I lost none of my purpose. None of my...commitment. In fact, I had determined, and I now pledged myself yet again—that before I did anything else, before I wrote another *word* I would absolutely do my part in the struggle. *(Beat)* And so I made a fateful decision, (one that I question to this day) and used my "Independent Labour" contacts...to get to Barcelona. *(Slight beat)* Except for one slight problem. My new wife was insisting on coming with me. *(Beat)* Now gentlemen...

YOUNG MAN: Sir!?

ORWELL: Pardon...me?

(ORWELL *turns and is now facing a delivery boy—who is standing the middle of the opened stage door, wide-eyed, his hands gripping a large box of groceries as he stares out at the audience.)*

YOUNG MAN: Delivery, sir. Your... *(Nervously, deer in headlights)* ...grocery delivery.

ORWELL: Oh. *(Realizing)* Oh, yes, of course, my... *(Beat)* I'm so sorry.
(With this, he starts for the YOUNG MAN, *only to briefly turn back to the audience.)*

ORWELL: One moment.
(Then, to the YOUNG MAN*)*
My grocery delivery, yes. Thank you. *(Calling out)* Miss Morrison??
(About to arrive, he holds up a finger to the YOUNG MAN.*)*
One moment. *(Then, offstage. Impatient)* Miss Morrison, please? We need to pay the young man. *(Beat; calling out, more impatiently)* Miss Morrison!

YOUNG MAN: I...actually...

ORWELL: What's that?

YOUNG MAN: I...
(He comes over and leans in to ORWELL, *whispering in his ear.)*

ORWELL: *(Impatiently)* Well, I can't, I— *(Again, calling, louder)* Miss Morrison! *(Then, to the audience.)* Be...
(Then, to YOUNG MAN*)* Would—
(Only to quickly turn around.)
Oh, for God's sake. How much is it?
(He takes out his wallet.)

YOUNG MAN: Twenty-two dollars and twelve cents.

*(*ORWELL *counts out the money.)*

ORWELL: Twenty...here, take this.
(He takes the box from the YOUNG MAN, *asking as he does)*
And you've brought what I asked you?

YOUNG MAN: I did, sir, yes. Everything you asked for.

ORWELL: Very well then. Thank you. And—

YOUNG MAN: You're—

ORWELL: Pardon me?

YOUNG MAN: *(Wide-eyed)* You're George Orwell?

ORWELL: I am, yes.

YOUNG MAN: *(Excited)* You wrote *Animal Farm*?

ORWELL: I did.

YOUNG MAN: Whoa. Doggies.

ORWELL: You've read it?

YOUNG MAN: Oh... *(Embarrassed)* Oh...no. *(Beat)* No.
(Sneaking a look at the audience)
My sister did. *(Then)* And she just loved it.

ORWELL: Your sister, 'eh?

YOUNG MAN: Yes.

ORWELL: But *you*..."didn't" read it?

YOUNG MAN: Um…

(At this, ORWELL looks out at the audience, bringing them in on the joke.)

ORWELL: I think maybe he's embarrassed. Are you embarrassed, young man?

YOUNG MAN: Yeah. I guess I am.

ORWELL: A children's book?

YOUNG MAN: Yes

ORWELL: *(To audience)* Isn't this wonderful? *(Then)* Well, now tell me something…*why* is it embarrassing?

YOUNG MAN: Well, like you said, it's a children's book.

ORWELL: And?

YOUNG MAN: And I'm not sure why I actually sat down to read it!

(And again ORWELL looks out.)

ORWELL: Yes, well I'm sure many in the audience would say the same.

(The audience laughs at this.)

ORWELL: But you…didn't…the story didn't speak to you?

YOUNG MAN: No, it did. Actually. That was…what I found surprising. Was that it did.

ORWELL: And believe me, an author could ask for nothing more. *(To YOUNG MAN)* Well, thank you. Oh. Actually…one other thing else. Would you give me a hand with something?

YOUNG MAN: *(Hesitant)* Sure.

ORWELL: What a fellow! Here, this way. *(To the audience)* Be… *(Then, to YOUNG MAN)* Over here, lad. I just need a hand with…

(By now they are offstage.)

ORWELL: *(Offstage)* So your sister, eh?

YOUNG MAN: *(Offstage)* That—

ORWELL: *(Offstage)* No...I'm just teasing. *(Then)* That's
it, right over here...if we could just...yes.

(By now ORWELL *and the* YOUNG MAN *have re-appeared
and are carrying a folding table between them.)*

ORWELL: That's it. And up!

*(*ORWELL *and the* YOUNG MAN *continue across the stage.)*

ORWELL: Right over here I think. Yes. That's it.
Right here. Oh, splendid. *(To audience)* Is this fellow
something? Here, let's give the young man a hand,
shall we?

(There is a round of applause.)

ORWELL: Oh, and...here. For your...efforts.

(And with this, ORWELL *once again opens his wallet,
pulling out yet another big bill—which the* YOUNG MAN
looks at with astonishment.)

YOUNG MAN: Gee, thanks!

ORWELL: My pleasure. And thank you!

*(*ORWELL *watches then as the* YOUNG MAN *makes his way
out, clearly enchanted by his boyish mixture of the naivete
and clumsiness.)*

ORWELL: Isn't he something? *(Beat, to the audience)*
Anyhow. *(Only to remember)* Oh! Actually...
(Here he looks down at the groceries at his feet)
...I'm sure you're wondering what I have here...
(Before bending down and quickly scooping them up)
...and how it applies to you.
(He then moves towards the table.)
Well, it doesn't...entirely. There is...
(Where he sets down the box)
For example...

(...And quickly fishes around inside it...)
...my newfound fondness for American whiskey.
(Only to pull out a bottle)
This...is entirely...for me.
(Which he immediately unscrews—and is about to take a drink...)
Well not entirely perhaps. I might, as the evening progresses...invite a companion.
(He knocks back a jolt)
But still, off the point. The point at the moment, this box, what's in it? And here I must tell you, my pleasures of this last week. And my impressions of America. *(Bursting out, impressed)* Good God!

VOICE: *(Hostile)* You prefer Russia???

(Again this interruption surprises ORWELL. *He'd thought he was saying something positive!)*

ORWELL: No, not at all.

VOICE: Then—

ORWELL: Sir, I would ask you again...please! Don't... *(He waits a moment. Then, when it's clear the man will allow him to continue—he does.)*
Though you do, in fact raise an interesting point. Which I'd been wondering how to describe. You see the people in England, "Albion"... *(He takes a moment.)*
...we didn't always *love* you Yanks...over there... during the war—

CARLOTTA: *(In hotel)* Oh for god—

ORWELL: There was actually a bit of how to put it? A bit of resentment...I guess you could say. The silk stockings for instance, the chocolates...the price of a picture show, our boys didn't have that. And so our girls, naturally...tended towards you. *(Beat)* Actually, that brings up an interesting point. Do you know who we liked best? Of the G Is? During the war?

CARLOTTA: You can't say that.

ORWELL: The Negroes.

CARLOTTA: It won't—

ORWELL: They seemed to understand us. *(Beat)* And we them.
(His tone when he says this is sad—almost as if he doesn't want to deliver this message.)

CARLOTTA: I'm…Mister Orwell, the people who are coming to see us…they…they're not necessarily liberal! They…don't—

ORWELL: In any case, the point I'm making, we didn't always get along. Our two people. Of course, in the larger sense we did. Roosevelt, Churchill, no question there. Hitler. But in the smaller sense, day to day, there was always…well, there was always a feeling—and I'm not saying everywhere, certainly not everywhere— but largely—there was often a feeling that you had too much…and we had too little.
(He knows he's treading on dangerous ground—and he's trying to be careful.)
And I often shared that feeling. *(Beat)* And now I've come here.
(By which he means he now has confirmed his feelings. though he's a trace sad about it.)
Now you must understand… *(Genuine)* …there is also an enormous debt—that we *all* feel.

CARLOTTA: Gee, thanks.

ORWELL: We know that your country, the *arsenal* as Churchill often called it, was central to our victory. That we could not have *had* our victory without you. *(Beat)* But… Well, put it this way, if you wonder why we are nationalizing our health care, our mines, our railways…and you are not—it is partly because of what we have suffered—that you have not.

(He lets this idea settle in.)
And to make this point, I thought, well now let's see
what you did without. And what we did without.

CARLOTTA: *(Short)* They don't compare.

ORWELL: After all, we both rationed, didn't we? Well,
what did you ration? And what did we?

CARLOTTA: Mister—

ORWELL: And how do they compare?

CARLOTTA: I just said, they don't! They... *(Exasperated)*
...look, I don't understand what you're doing here!

ORWELL: Watch. You'll see. *(Then again, to the audience)*
So...to start with, what was rationed?

CARLOTTA: We haven't forgotten, believe me.

ORWELL: Well, here in America, as you all know, you
rationed petrol, fuel oil, sugar, coffee, meats, canned
goods, and, curiously I found, typewriters. And you
did so using ration books, one red book, one blue. The
red book, with sixty-four coupons per month was for
meats. The blue book with forty-eight coupons was for
canned goods.

CARLOTTA: Which was only a fraction of what we
rationed.

ORWELL: And it allowed for a family of four...to
continue—though in limited supply...to buy steak
(He pulls out a slab of beef.) ...cheeses... *(He adds a few
wedges.)*

CARLOTTA: *(Outraged)* But we started with *more*, don't
you see??

ORWELL: ...a variety of canned goods
(He puts a store of cans on the table.)

CARLOTTA: So what you're doing here isn't fair!

ORWELL: …not to mention the array of things that were *not* rationed…among them, bread, bananas, citrus.
(He now adds mightily to the pile, turning to CARLOTTA.*)*
Oh, I think it's quite fair.
(Before turning back to the audience)
And I should add—yours was over by 1945.
(At this point, he looks at the audience and at the table, a fair number of items stacked up in a heap.)
Ours, beginning before you, in 1940, continues to this day.
(He waits for a moment, sure his point is made.)
And to this day we are limited, this per individual…to two ounces of bacon or ham per fortnight.
(He takes out a tiny sliver.)

CARLOTTA: That's two ounces?

ORWELL: An ounce and a half of cheese…per week.
(He adds a tiny clump.)

ORWELL: Two ounces of cooking fat…per week.
(A small tin now.)

CARLOTTA: That—

ORWELL: An egg…a week.
(It's just that, a single egg.)

ORWELL: Three packets of dried milk…weekly.
(He adds three packs of dry-flake milk.)

CARLOTTA: *(Hushed)* My god.

ORWELL: And a sweet.
(At the end of the table, he now puts a gumdrop—which stands alone.)
This is not to mention the clothing in our country which is also rationed. As is the furniture. And since the war ended we have even added two *new* commodities to our ration list. Bread. And potatoes.
(He breaks off a hunk of bread, and gathers three potatoes, the collection of food a tiny fraction of what the American

items look like at the other end of the table.)
It is now *three* years after the war. And for a decade we
have lived with this. Every man, woman, and child.
And the result is that today the children are quite
short. *(Beat)* The children I see…are indeed…"quite"
short. *(Beat)* So… *(Gently)* Socialism… *(Here his voice
softens a bit—as if to say "it's different, isn't it?")*

ORWELL: It's not what…

(When suddenly the lights return to the hotel.)

CARLOTTA: But that's not the point!

ORWELL: Of course, it—

CARLOTTA: It doesn't matter that we…that… *(She is
stumbling—yet forceful.)* …you are suggesting in some
way that there is a difference between us. And not only
is that not helpful in our task here—which is *to sell your
book*…but again, it misses the point! Yes, for this brief
moment, it's true. Your country is not as well provided.
But do you really mean…I mean, my goodness, do
you—

ORWELL: I—

CARLOTTA: We are talking about our century here! We
are talking about the currents of history. We are talking
about where we're likely to *be* a hundred years from
now. And what you have done in *Animal Farm*, what
you have done so brilliantly in *Animal Farm*, is to show
us where we mustn't go! *That's* the story. Not this
moment. Not this temporary, transitory moment. What
you are confusing, and I hope you'll forgive me for
speaking so freely, but what you are confusing are the
challenges of today…in the first years after what has to
be called the most destructive war in human history…
with the choices of a civilization! *(Beat)* We are in the
midst of choosing. Mister Orwell! And we must not
choose based on our panic of the moment. We must

choose based on a *broad* vision…a *long* vision… *(Beat, reverent)* …of what is best for the human spirit.

ORWELL: The human spirit.

CARLOTTA: The human spirit, yes! That aspect that allows us to advance as we have. To cast aside kings. To leave slavery behind. The human spirit! Yes!

(ORWELL looks at CARLOTTA with some pleasure. and admiration.)

ORWELL: An element which you seem to have in some measure.

CARLOTTA: I'm just saying—

ORWELL: I understand what you're saying. And I have real sympathy for it. I do. But at this moment, Miss Morrison…and this is what you can't understand living where you do…at this moment, people are dying. Of starvation. We are currently feeding…I wonder if you know this…we are currently feeding *half* of Europe. *(Beat)* And we are currently feeding them on a diet of fourteen hundred calories a day. *(Beat)* Do you see? *(Beat)* There is no "history" …when people are dying of want. *(Beat)* But I do understand what you're saying. And I'll bear it in mind. If you'll do me a favor.

CARLOTTA: What?

ORWELL: That part that came next. That part about Spain. What did you think of it?
(He is smiling, "pleased" with himself.)

CARLOTTA: I—

ORWELL: Didn't see that coming, did they? *(Loud)* WHACK!
(He is suddenly back in front of the audience— enthusiastically telling an adventure story, as if to a group of boy scouts. He is giddy!)
Here I'd been not six months in the country—and

bang—out of action. I'm afraid the trenches built to safeguard the Spaniard, which did a very good job of it, were in no way fit for a long-legged Englishman. At least not one prone to day-dreaming. Which is what I was doing one morning, gazing absently across a hillside, morning cigarette in hand, when suddenly I saw a blinding flash, heard a loud bang, felt what seemed an electric shock across my entire body—and then found myself flat on my back. Without a voice. *(Then, almost instantly, still "up"...)*
At least that was the message I was given, the prognosis as it were, of the first doctor I saw, a rather square-faced internist in Lerida who told me my "larynx was broken" ...and I would never speak again. *(Again, a pause—but just for a moment)*
Which came as news to my wife Eileen, who was immediately at my side, sending back messages to my parents saying "my progress was wonderful"— without going into details of what I was making my progress from. And in a sense I *was* making progress; in no small sense because of her. Eileen at my side, I have no doubt, saved my life. *(Adding, almost instantly)*
So gentlemen, for those—

(When suddenly the lights come up on the hotel.)

CARLOTTA: *(Sharp)* Did you love her?

ORWELL: *(Thrown, angry)* Pardon??

CARLOTTA: I'm sorry to interrupt you, but your wife. *(Beat)* Did you love her?

ORWELL: Well, of course I did!

CARLOTTA: Good.

ORWELL: Why do you ask me that?

CARLOTTA: *(Beat)* There are times that I wonder.

ORWELL: Based on what? What...what have I ever said that would make you *ask* such a thing???

CARLOTTA: It's not what you've said. It's what you haven't said.

ORWELL: What?

CARLOTTA: Those words. That you "loved her". *(Beat)* It would be good, during your talk, if you mentioned that.

(ORWELL is struck—truly stunned. a moment passes.)

ORWELL: Yes. I will.

CARLOTTA: Good. It will... *(She decides not to say it. Saying instead, repeating actually...)* Good.

(And again ORWELL turns, shifting once more to the auditorium—where again he's in the midst of his story.)

ORWELL: In any case, from Lerida we went on to Barcelona, where we were soon faced with a nightmare. The organization I'd been allied with, the whites, if you will, the "non-communists", were being arrested as deserters!
(He becomes bitter as he remembers this—though tries to remain "light".)
I learned this most pointedly when Eileen came up to me in the lobby of our hotel, I was still recuperating, and whispered to me tightly, "get out!" She did so with a broad smile on her face, her hand firmly gripping my elbow as she led me to an elevator, repeating, quietly, because I was in total shock when she said this— "get out". It seems that the group I was being associated with had been arrested as deserters, several shot, some executed, the entire group declared "illegal" by the government of Catalonia. And why?
(This last he says with some heat, his outrage starting to boil.)
Because the grand poohbah himself, Josef Stalin, couldn't give a good goddam about what we were fighting for. The Republic. He was interested in the

Left. In *controlling* the Left. And so it was that an
organization absolutely *critical* to that struggle—
one that had supplied it with literally *thousands* of
fighters—could, in the *midst* of that battle—be declared
illegal.
(The wound still burns. He shakes as he says it.)
And the men that I fought with, people who had
risked their lives for a country that was hundreds
if not thousands of miles away from their own…
could, *also* in the midst of that battle, be referred to…
and Stalin and his henchmen referred to us this way
repeatedly—as Fascists! *(He is irate at this.)* If you can
believe it. Fascists!!! For God's sake! *(Boiling with rage)*
Well, I have never forgotten that. And I will never
forgive it. *(Then, ruthlessly…)* And from that moment
on, I began thinking of *Animal Farm*…of Snowball,
and Napoleon…and a way of describing what Josef
Stalin… *(Beat, moved)* …what that mass-murderer, Josef
Stalin…had done to our cause—to Socialism. *(Beat)* I—

VOICE: He exposed it, that's all. He showed it for what
it was!

*(At this, ORWELL turns on the man—not shocked this time;
but instead quietly, and angrily, determined.)*

ORWELL: No. My friend. He corrupted it. And turned it
into something that you and your friends can so easily
defame. *(Beat)* And when we return, I'll explain what I
mean by that…
(Then, with a smile to the audience)
In the meantime, I wonder if we might take a short
break. And as I say, when we return…actually, when
we return, I'll start in with your questions.

(The lights come up on the hotel.)

CARLOTTA: Your *questions*???

ORWELL: I've decided to take questions, yes.
(He turns back to the audience, bowing.)
Thank you.

CARLOTTA: *(Outraged)* From the audience?

(By now the lights have faded on the audience, as ORWELL *makes his way to the room.)*

ORWELL: Do you have another suggestion?

CARLOTTA: In the middle...you're going to start taking questions now??? In the middle of the tour?
(She is truly incredulous at this.)

ORWELL: Why not?

CARLOTTA: Why... *(Then)* ...because...it...

ORWELL: What?

CARLOTTA: We have faced criticism!

ORWELL: That's right.

CARLOTTA: From this fellow, for instance. And he's not *alone* out there.

ORWELL: Which is why I'd prefer his not be the only voice we hear.

(Long pause. CARLOTTA *is truly dumb-founded by his suggestion.)*

CARLOTTA: What *type* of questions? What... And how do you plan on gathering them?

ORWELL: Well, that will be your job, won't it?

CARLOTTA: My *what*???

ORWELL: Come, Miss Morrison. Don't be shocked. It will be fun. *(Sly smile)* Don't you think?

CARLOTTA: I... *(At a loss)* ...I have no idea what...I don't know how to *do* this.

ORWELL: You will. *(Beat)* I'm sure in due time, you will. *(Beat)* In the meantime...

(He holds up a bottle, insouciant)
...drink?

(Here CARLOTTA *stares for a moment, not knowing how to respond. Then, suddenly, unexpectedly...)*

CARLOTTA: Sure. Why not?

ORWELL: There you are!

(And instantly, before CARLOTTA *can change her mind,* ORWELL *immediately starts to pour—bringing her a glass.)*

ORWELL: Now you're getting it.
(He then goes back for his own.)

CARLOTTA: Mister... *(Beat, reminding herself)* ...Blair?

ORWELL: Eric.

CARLOTTA: Eric. *(Beat)* No, never mind.

ORWELL: What?

CARLOTTA: I was just going to ask something...which I now think it would be foolish to ask.

ORWELL: What? Please *(Beat)* Ask.

(And with this CARLOTTA *turns back, taking a moment.)*

CARLOTTA: All that you've said. All... *(New idea)* These ideas that you have. About the miners. The poor. Spain. *(Slight beat)* Do you truly believe it?

*(*ORWELL *turns to* CARLOTTA—*realizing the seriousness of the question. That she is really trying to understand.)*

ORWELL: I do, Miss Morrison. I—

CARLOTTA: Carlotta.

(And as soon as CARLOTTA *says this,* ORWELL *realizes it isn't a correction she's making. Or a mistake. It's an invitation.)*

ORWELL: Carlotta. *(Beat)* I do, yes. I believe what I say...very...much. *(Then, abruptly)* But now, on to other things. *(Raising his glass)* Cheers.

(*And here* ORWELL *waits—wondering if/how* CARLOTTA *will respond. And finally, a trace mystified perhaps, she indeed raises her glass back.*)

CARLOTTA: Cheer—

(*Only to instantly stop herself—which in turns stops* ORWELL.)

CARLOTTA: Actually, one other thing. And I'm not sure how to say this. But the fact that I'm here. And not...as your publicist...but just...as me...

(*This last* CARLOTTA *says meaningfully, letting a moment pass—wanting to make certain* ORWELL *understands what she's saying.*)

CARLOTTA: Does that *please* you?

(*And* ORWELL *can only stare back at* CARLOTTA. *For the longest moment. Of course it pleases him. He's in love with her!*)

ORWELL: Well, of course, it does. It does very much.

CARLOTTA: Well then, why haven't you asked about me? (*Beat*) More, I mean? Than you have?
(*There is the slightest hint of disappointment in her voice.*)

ORWELL: I... (*Flustered*) Well—

CARLOTTA: What I like. Where I'm from. (*Beat*) Why I think the way I do.

ORWELL: Well, we've established that, haven't we? You're a cousin of Hemingway's!

(*This last* ORWELL *says as a joke. But* CARLOTTA *isn't amused.*)

CARLOTTA: More than that. (*Beat*) The fact that I've fought for you. For instance. That when my bosses said you couldn't do this...I said that you *could*. That with me at your side...you could. (*Beat*) Does that...does that mean anything to you?

(ORWELL *is stunned.*)

ORWELL: It does, yes. It means a great deal.

(Beat. CARLOTTA *stares at* ORWELL. *Wondering if he's being truthful.)*

CARLOTTA: Good. *(Beat)* I'm glad to hear that. I have great faith in you, Mister… "Eric". *(Beat)* Great faith. *(And with that, she smiles. And takes a moment. Then raises her glass.)*
Cheers.

(And ORWELL, *now a little cooler, raises his glass as well.)*

ORWELL: Yes. *(Beat)* Cheers.

(Broadly smiling, CARLOTTA *then takes a drink—only to nearly spit it out, the taste of the alcohol so new to her. This in turn causes* ORWELL *to laugh just a little…)*

ORWELL: Easy now.

(…Clearly delighted. As the lights…slowly fade…to black.)

END ACT ONE

ACT TWO

(CARLOTTA *stands near the doorway shaking her head.*
ORWELL *is looking back at her. It is the next day. She is
annoyed. Resentful)*

CARLOTTA: You said you would go back out.

ORWELL: I know.

CARLOTTA: So you shouldn't have just *left* them!

ORWELL: I didn't.

CARLOTTA: You did!

ORWELL: I sent you out. *(Beat)* And you explained that I
was indisposed.

(ORWELL *looks back at* CARLOTTA—*clearly uncomfortable
with what he has done; but nonetheless not backing down.
She, remains resentful.)*

CARLOTTA: That man, for instance, our critic, he was
very angry with me.

ORWELL: I won't do it again.

CARLOTTA: And he got others to be angry as well. They
were not nice to me!

ORWELL: I understand. I… *(Resolute)* It won't happen
again. *(Beat)* I promise.

(*At this,* CARLOTTA *can only stare at* ORWELL, *realizing
in that moment that he will not say any more. That he is*

*determined. And finally, taking a deep breath, she turns
away; giving up.)*

CARLOTTA: Well, we're off in... *(She looks down at her
watch.)* ...two hours.

ORWELL: What's next?

CARLOTTA: Utica.

ORWELL: Which?

CARLOTTA: Utica. New York. A small city in New York.
(Then) And Mister...

ORWELL: Eric.

CARLOTTA: Eric. I rea...

*(About to say "really think you should", CARLOTTA
suddenly stops herself, thinking better of what she was about
to say. After all, it's clear to her by now—ORWELL isn't
going to change.)*

CARLOTTA: ...no, never mind.

ORWELL: What were you going to say?

CARLOTTA: Nothing, I... *(Dismissing it)* ...nothing.
*(She looks at him for a moment—and then remembers
something else she'd wanted to say.)*
Actually, there *is* something I wanted to ask you.

*(ORWELL nods, indicating CARLOTTA should. She is trying
to let go of her anger.)*

CARLOTTA: Why... *(Beat)* No, I don't want to ask that.
It's too big a subject.

ORWELL: What?

CARLOTTA: I'll save it for the train.

ORWELL: What? We have two hours.

(Beat)

CARLOTTA: Why…? *(Re-calibrating)* I'm trying to think how best to phrase this. What makes you *feel* the way you do?

ORWELL: I—

CARLOTTA: Actually, that's not the right question. What… *(Then)* Here, perhaps this is better. Why does one person *care*… *(Beat)* …where another person doesn't?

(At this ORWELL *eyes* CARLOTTA *for a moment, not knowing how to answer.)*

ORWELL: Well, that *is* a big question. One that I'm not sure how to answer. *(Beat)* Though it's not unlike what you asked yesterday.

CARLOTTA: I'm—

ORWELL: And I'll attempt to answer it…again… *(Beat)* …on one condition. That you come and sit next to me.

CARLOTTA: No.

ORWELL: No?

(Beat)

CARLOTTA: No. I think—

ORWELL: Try not to.

(Beat)

CARLOTTA: *(Letting him down gently)* I shouldn't.

(Beat)

ORWELL: Oh.

CARLOTTA: Not that I don't want to. *(Beat)* I *do*…in part. But I suspect…for our… *(Beat)* …that I shouldn't.

ORWELL: I see.

CARLOTTA: However… *(This last she says quickly, taking a pause, smiling.)* …and what is the word you use?

"Assuage". *(Beat)* Perhaps I might sit closer to you...
(She smiles.) ...and see how *that* works.

(ORWELL smiles as well, brightened by CARLOTTA's "sass".)

ORWELL: Yes, all right. Let's see how that works.

(CARLOTTA comes over. And sits.)

CARLOTTA: Better?

ORWELL: Not...

(CARLOTTA moves over a bit.)

CARLOTTA: Now?

ORWELL: Getting there.

CARLOTTA: Well, let's leave it at this then...for the moment...shall we? And see how we feel in a bit. *(Again she smiles.)* Now then.

ORWELL: Yes?

CARLOTTA: What I was saying before. About politics. Why—

ORWELL: Oh.

CARLOTTA: And you're right, I did...it *is* like I asked yesterday. Because I'm still confused by it. *(Beat)* I...I don't... After all, you're not a *poor* person. You don't come from a *poor* family. Why do such questions concern you? Why—I mean, you say you were "obsessed" with poverty. *(Holding out her hands)* Why?

(Beat. ORWELL is taken by CARLOTTA's question.)

ORWELL: It's an interesting question.

CARLOTTA: Do you know?
(Meaning "do you understand what I'm driving at?")

ORWELL: I do, yes. *(Beat)* And I'm not sure I can answer it. *(He thinks a moment.)* But I'll try. *(Beat, another moment)* I… *(Only to reach for the bottle)* Do you want a drink?

CARLOTTA: No. *(Beat)* Thank you. And I don't…and I'm not sure you should either.

(But it's already too late. ORWELL *is already pouring.)*

ORWELL: It has something to do with my upbringing…I should think. After all, I was charity. *(Slight beat)* At Cyprian, Eton. My family couldn't pay for me. And I was made aware of that. *(Bitter)* Every day I was there. *(It is almost like he is going back in time, remembering his childhood pain.)* So that's part of it. I did…well, I was going to say I did know poverty. I didn't. But I did know wealth. *(Again, bitter)* And I didn't always like it. *(Beat)* But yes, there were many like me. Many… what,"charity" boys. Very few with…with real… *(Struggling to say "knowledge of poverty", he finds that he can't. He feels like a poseur.)* So what did I…? *(Beat, mystified)* I don't know. *(Then, trying to shift the attention)* What about you?

CARLOTTA: Well, I told you—

ORWELL: You've never…when you pass a poor man, a beggar, do you ever think how he came to be the way he is?

CARLOTTA: No. *(Beat)* No, I just try to get by him.

*(*ORWELL *laughs—amused by* CARLOTTA's *callousness.)*

ORWELL: That's all. Just get by?

CARLOTTA: Yes, I—

ORWELL: He's in your way?

CARLOTTA: Well, it's not so bad as that.

ORWELL: You don't want to be inconvenienced.

*(*CARLOTTA *stares at* ORWELL, *miffed.)*

CARLOTTA: We were talking about you. Not me.

ORWELL: *(Uneasy)* You're right.

CARLOTTA: It does...trouble me. But it doesn't... monopolize my thinking. As it seems to do you.

ORWELL: Yes.

CARLOTTA: And I wonder why that is.

ORWELL: You or me?

CARLOTTA: You.

ORWELL: Well, as I say—

CARLOTTA: There are many people who were poor. Who suffered poverty. Deprivation. Who go on to write about *other* things. *(Slight beat)* Beauty. Escaping from poverty. *(Beat)* You, instead, keep yourself in. *(Beat)* And now you're writing about politics of a different stripe. Tyranny. Oppression. And I wonder why *that* is. *(Slight beat)* What makes you write the way you do? What moves you?

ORWELL: *(Flummoxed)* Well, I...the injustice.

CARLOTTA: *(Pouncing)* Which you alone are attuned to? Doesn't everyone see that injustice? Why do you choose to write about it—where others do not?

ORWELL: Well...I—

CARLOTTA: Does it...
(She stops herself suddenly.)

ORWELL: Pardon?

CARLOTTA: No, nothing.

ORWELL: You were going to say something.

CARLOTTA: No, I shouldn't.

ORWELL: Go ahead.

(Beat)

CARLOTTA: Well, I just wonder if it doesn't make you *feel* better.

ORWELL: Yes, of course it does.

CARLOTTA: In a way other things do not.

ORWELL: Yes.

CARLOTTA: By that I mean... *(Being careful)* ...there is some discomfort in you. Inside. And this...fixation... helps to distract from that.

(The minute CARLOTTA *says this* ORWELL *recognizes the truth of it. And immediately seeks to create distance.)*

ORWELL: *(Outraged)* That is the reason that I write about politics?

CARLOTTA: Yes.

ORWELL: That is the reason I write about injustice???

CARLOTTA: Yes.

ORWELL: *(Angry, frightened, sputtering)* Because I have... because there's a part of me...

(Slight pause)

CARLOTTA: Yes.

ORWELL: No! *(He is furious.)* No, I write about what I do because of what I see. *(Then)* But look, this is...you're right, this *is* a big topic. Too big perhaps. Perhaps we...

CARLOTTA: Could—

ORWELL: Actually. I think we should talk about the tour. Some changes we...I think we have to make some changes.

CARLOTTA: *(Caught off)* Oh?

ORWELL: The questions for instance.

CARLOTTA: What about them?

ORWELL: I'd like you to ask them.

CARLOTTA: You...what???

ORWELL: I'd like you to ask them.

CARLOTTA: No, I—

ORWELL: Rather than have the audience address me directly…which is not a good thing; I think we've seen that—I'd like to collect their questions and have you pose them to me.

CARLOTTA: I…again, I'm not certain I understand the reason for the questions.

ORWELL: Well, we've been over that—

CARLOTTA: But I certainly don't understand how that… *(Stumbling)* …how I'll—

ORWELL: It will be more interesting, that's all. And look, the first half will still be as it is. And much of the second as well. I'll still…and even in the second half; for much of the second half, it will still be pretty much the same. I'll still—

(Quickly ORWELL *turns, facing the audience. He is once again on stage.)*

ORWELL: The English language. *(Beat)* Let's talk more about that.

CARLOTTA: Oh god.

(While CARLOTTA *remains in the hotel.)*

ORWELL: After all, it's a thing we both share, isn't it? In a sense?
(He moves across the stage, by now with much greater command than he had at the start. He is really engaging.)
And whether we share it in all its particulars we most definitely share a central problem with it. It is no longer what it once was. It is changing. And it is not changing for the better. *(Slight beat)* I am speaking here in particular of the written word. Which has been debased. Which—

CARLOTTA: But—

ORWELL: *(To* CARLOTTA*)* And then I'll go on to *Animal Farm*, yes?

(Here the lights return to the hotel, as ORWELL *turns to* CARLOTTA*.)*

ORWELL: You've wanted me to recap *Animal Farm*, didn't you? Didn't you say you wanted me to recap *Animal Farm*?

CARLOTTA: I did.

ORWELL: So...
(And again he turns out—once again to the crowd.)
Actually, I've been asked to...how to put it...review the high points...shall we say of the book. So for those who have read it, bear with me. For those who have not...
(Here he retrieves an easel with the image of Animal Farm *on it.)*
...the book, *Animal Farm*, what's it about? Well, to start with— *(Pointing)* —a farm. On it—not surprisingly—a farmer. A Farmer Jones. A drunk. Actually, I should amend that. A man who "likes" his drink. *(To* CARLOTTA*)* Yes?
(He then returns to the audience, once again on a roll, wholly involved, truly enjoying himself!)
In any case, along with Farmer Jones, there are a variety of animals, above all a group of pigs—and chief among these, at least to start with, a boar a prize boar—Old Major. Who has an epiphany. One night he has an epiphany and he calls all the animals together, the animals of what is called "Manor Farm", to tell them about it. To start with, he reminds them, they are miserable. There can be no doubt about that. And the reason for that misery—and this his epiphany—is humans. Human beings are the source of animal misery and they will never be happy he tells them,

truly *happy*—animals, that is—until the people are overthrown.

CARLOTTA: Good.

ORWELL: And then almost immediately he dies. No sooner has Old Major given his speech and held his meeting than he dies.

VOICE: *(Calling out)* Good riddance!

(ORWELL smiles at the interjection.)

ORWELL: But his ideas do not die with him. Instead they are taken up by a pair of younger pigs—young, *ambitious* pigs—Snowball and Napoleon—who not only embellish on Old Major's creed—but give it a name— "Animalism ".

CARLOTTA: Very good.

ANOTHER VOICE: Communism!

ORWELL: And not only give it a name, but come up with a set of Commandments...seven of them... *(At this point he goes offstage...)*

ORWELL: ...along with a song—*Beasts of England*—

(...Where ORWELL meets CARLOTTA, the two of them then returning with a blackboard on which the seven commandments have been written.)

ORWELL: ...which they teach every night in secret meetings for the entire farm. These Commandments, among them, "whoever goes on two legs is an enemy" "no animal shall wear clothes" ...and above all... "all animals are equal"... *(Pointing out each as he mentions them.)* ...has soon got the entire farm in an uproar, the animals wild with self-righteousness, until the next time Farmer Jones predictably forgets a feeding—he is after all a drunk—the animals, furious at their mistreatment, break into open rebellion! Break into open, *wild rebellion! (He is clearly enjoying himself.)* And

this rebellion, which includes chasing Farmer Jones
from the farm, is soon followed by an even bigger
battle—this time with Farmer Jones returning with
armed men—where again the animals are victorious...
and again the men are chased away...until, much to
their amazement, the animals suddenly realize the
farm belongs to them! *(Now wide-eyed with amazement)*
For their use alone! There are no people among them!
*(His voice here has taken on a sense of "wonder" at their
surprise. he is reveling in the "acting.")* And they rename
it...this place where they've spent their whole lives...
"Animal Farm".

(Beat)

CARLOTTA: Yes. Fabulous. *That's* where you'll have
them.

(CARLOTTA is again seen from the hotel.)

ORWELL: Only to discover that their leaders have begun
to fight with each other. Snowball and Napoleon,
in particular, each want control, and Napoleon, the
shrewder of the two, has secretly trained a pack of
vicious dogs which he soon *turns* on Snowball—
chasing him away. He then follows this act by taking
credit for all of Snowball's ideas—chief among these
the building of a *windmill*—expunges Snowball from
the official history, and employs yet another pig, this
one named Squealer, to fine tune a new message for
the farm. From now on, he tells them, the pigs *will
sleep in the farmhouse!* *(This last he says belligerently,
"playing" the character.)* This of course is in direct
contravention of yet another commandment. But no
matter. "The pigs will now sleep in the farmhouse".
That was decided. This decision is then followed by
others, a series of others, until finally, the windmill
completed but their foodstuffs near vanished,
Napoleon makes an announcement. It is necessary, he

tells them, to sell the farm's timber to the humans next door. This is supposedly to purchase the machinery necessary to run the windmill, but the real reason is he wants to buy whiskey…whiskey so that he and his inner circle; along with the humans from next door, can cavort, drunkenly, into the night. And the animals…demoralized, disoriented, dispirited, fall into despair. How can this be? How can it be that their Commandments, Commandments that had once taken up an entire wall of the barn have now been *expunged*? All save one, that is. The one reading "all animals are equal" is still there. But now with an addition. *(Sadly, as if one of the animals.)* All animals are indeed equal… *(Then, after a moment.)* …but some…and here the addition… "some…are more equal than others". *(Beat)* And there the tale…as the poet might once have said… comes to an end.

(With this, ORWELL *ends his story—only to immediately meet with an outcry.)*

A VOICE FROM UTICA: So how can you be a Communist?

(Which shocks ORWELL.*)*

ORWELL: I'm not.

A VOICE FROM UTICA: Then how—

ORWELL: May I…stop you for a second? *(Here he quickly turns to the others , trying to quickly regain control.)* As you recall, I've asked everyone to…provide questions. And I'd now like to ask my associate, Miss Morrison… *(He turns to the wings, calling out loudly)* …Miss *Carlotta Morrison,* to come out and join me. *(He continues to look into the wings.)* She has your questions. And she and I will—

A VOICE FROM UTICA: *(Insistent)* But I didn't have this
question then. I do now. How can you be a Communist
after writing that book?

ORWELL: Again... *(Once again, calling out to* CARLOTTA,
desperate) Miss Morrison?!? *(Only to turn back to the man,
trying to remain calm)* Again, I am *not* a Communist.
And I hope through this...question period...I can make
that point clearly. *(He then shares with the others.)*
Also, I should say that...if it turns out that...I have
not answered your questions fully...that you remain
intrigued, or confused...

(And here, finally, CARLOTTA *comes out—a stack of
questions held in her hand.)*

ORWELL: ...perhaps we'll have time to take a few more
directly from the stage. *(Beat)* But I'd like to at least
start with...

*(*CARLOTTA *soon arranges her chair, placing it directly
opposite* ORWELL's—*the two chairs facing each other.)*

ORWELL: ...if you'll allow us... *(He then goes to his chair.)*
...to start with your questions.

(Until finally CARLOTTA *and* ORWELL *are settled, and he
then nods his head—only to interrupt her the moment she
starts to speak.)*

ORWELL: Again, Carlotta Morrison, my assistant.

(Here CARLOTTA *looks at* ORWELL *crossly, not liking her
title.)*

ORWELL: My associate. My associate. *(Then, promoting
her)* My colleague.

*(*CARLOTTA *then looks down at her lap, taking the first of
her questions.)*

CARLOTTA: *(Nervous)* Um...well, to start with...
(Reading) ..."How do you like Utica?"

ORWELL: Pardon?

CARLOTTA: The question...is... "How do you like Utica?"

ORWELL: I...very well. Very...lovely. *(To audience)* You have a lovely city. Very... *(To* CARLOTTA, *then, unsure)* That's the question?

CARLOTTA: Yes.

ORWELL: Um...yes. I—actually, we arrived a little after four...this afternoon, so...I can't say I've seen too much of it. But what I *have* seen, yes, absolutely, very...very lovely.

*(*ORWELL *looks at* CARLOTTA, *nodding his head. Next question)*

CARLOTTA: How can—

A VOICE FROM UTICA: *(Belligerent)* You been to "East Side"?

ORWELL: I—

A VOICE FROM UTICA: The slums?

ORWELL: Again, please, I would...ask...that...uh...we proceeded in the way...
(He nods towards CARLOTTA, *and her stack—before continuing.)*

ORWELL: ...but, no, as I say, I haven't seen very *much* of the city. But what I have seen...on the way over, from the train station, the road over, the avenue, the...it seems very lovely.
(Again he looks at CARLOTTA.)

CARLOTTA: How—

A VOICE FROM UTICA: So how does that square with "socialism"?

ORWELL: *(Losing his temper)* The one has nothing to do with the other! The... *(Then)* Please!

(Even after this, ORWELL *is tempted to continue answering—but instead he merely looks at* CARLOTTA. *And when the man doesn't continue, she is able to proceed.)*

CARLOTTA: How…and this is related I think. Though you've already answered I believe "How can you call yourself a Socialist…and write a book like *Animal Farm?*

ORWELL: I've answered that.

*(*CARLOTTA *nods. Then starts for another question.)*

CARLOTTA: Do—

ORWELL: *(Again losing his temper)* I mean, that's the subject of this entire talk, isn't it? *Animal Farm* is a book about totalitarianism. Stalinism in particular. It is actually a recapitulation of the entire Russian Revolution. It's doesn't…I don't—

ANOTHER UTICAN VOICE: *(Interjecting, helpfully)* The pigs are people.

ORWELL: *(Lashing out)* Pardon?

ANOTHER UTICAN VOICE: They're trying to be like people. Walking on their hind legs. The pigs.
(He looks at the questioner and realizes she is trying to be helpful.)

ORWELL: They're walking on their hind legs, correct.

ANOTHER UTICAN VOICE: Can't tell 'em apart.

ORWELL: That's…yes. *(To audience)* The lady is talking about the end of the book. At which point, if you'll recall, the pigs are wearing clothing, walking on their hind legs, and have become indistinguishable from humans.

A VOICE FROM UTICA: Which is socialism.

ORWELL: No, that—

A VOICE FROM UTICA: That's the way it works, isn't it?

ORWELL: No! Please! It is not a function of Socialism
that distorts the ideal. It is a function of *Communism*.
It is a function of a single, hierarchical structure—the
Communist Party, in this case the Communist Party of
the Soviet Union that *perverts* the idea of Socialism and
makes it *indistinguishable* from capitalism. Or, I should
say, *worse* than capitalism. The farm animals, after all,
starve!!!
*(This last he says loudly—brutally—harshly. He is barely
able to control himself. He is clearly irate.)*
But it is not Socialism that makes them starve. It is
not…and Socialism, as we see in England today can
exist in a *free* society. It can even exist, one might argue,
in a capitalist society—some parts socialist, some part
capitalist—and bring enormous benefits to people! It—

A VOICE FROM UTICA: It'll come to the same.

ORWELL: It will *not* come to the same. *(Repeating the
phrase)* "It will come—" It will not! Good… *(About
to say "god, man!", he instead mutters.)* Come to the…
(Continuing, under his breath) It will not. *(Then, again,
as if to convince himself)* It will not. *(He gathers himself.
Then)* Next question.

THIRD UTICAN VOICE: How—

ORWELL: Please! I must ask that we refrain…from
shouting out questions. Miss Morrison?

CARLOTTA: "What about Russia?"

ORWELL: *(Short)* What *about* Russia?

CARLOTTA: That's—

ORWELL: We are *preoccupied* with Russia. We… And
in a sense, of course, it's understandable. But we are
pre-*occupied*! You here in America in particular. I mean,
good God, when you think of Socialism, you think of
Stalin, and I want to de-couple the two! Don't you see?
Free one from the other. And celebrate the possibility of

men living together in a better way. That is my point.
That is my *entire* point. *(Angrier)* That I am a socialist.
That I am *proud* to be a socialist! *(He is breathing fire
now, truly enraged.)*

CARLOTTA: Could—

ORWELL: *(Startled)* Please?

CARLOTTA: Could I…interject for a moment?

ORWELL: I'd rather that you didn't actually.

CARLOTTA: *(Herself angry)* I think what the audience
is saying…so long as we're considering it is that it is
difficult to de-couple the two. Stalinism and Socialism.
That they're connected. In some way. Inextricably. And
that it's a mistake…a terrible mistake, to ignore that
fact. *(Beat)* How do you answer that?

*(ORWELL stares at CARLOTTA, astonished that she would
ask such an impertinent question. And he takes a moment to
respond.)*

ORWELL: I reject it. I say that that's the kind of
argument that's been used throughout history to
resist progress. That the kings and queens used that
argument to resist democracy. *(Beat)* I *reject* that
argument. As I suspect many in our audience do as
well. *(Here he looks at the audience, challenging them.)*

CARLOTTA: I—

ORWELL: Next question.

CARLOTTA: Perhaps—

ORWELL: I said next question!

*(Suddenly the lights change, and CARLOTTA and ORWELL
are in the hotel—she on the defensive, he still quite angry.
Their conversation from the auditorium continues without
missing a beat. It is fast, intense.)*

CARLOTTA: No reason to be angry.

ORWELL: That was not my understanding!

CARLOTTA: What wasn't?

ORWELL: That you would ask such questions. That you would challenge me so!

(CARLOTTA *is getting angry as well.*)

CARLOTTA: You'd rather I shut off my brain.

ORWELL: Not at all.

CARLOTTA: Why wouldn't I challenge you?

ORWELL: Because we want to control the proceedings! *(Slight beat)* Because we want…I mean, correct me if I'm wrong, darling, but I thought you were concerned about the response we were getting. About whether the audience stayed on our side. About whether we would sell books! *(Slight beat)* Is that not a concern of yours?

CARLOTTA: It is.

ORWELL: So then, how can you find my complaint confusing??? *(Slight beat)* When you take issue with me, the audience does not know *who* to believe. When you take issue, they assume it's part of the discussion. That I *want* you to take issue. That I, in fact, *share* your concern. And I do not! Stalinism and Socialism are not at all interchangeable. And I would like you to help relate that message by not *questioning* it.

CARLOTTA: But I'm not sure I agree with you.

ORWELL: All well and good! I would simply ask that you reserve your confusion for our private conversation! At which point, I will be more than happy, as you should know by now, *more* than happy…to continue enlightening you.

CARLOTTA: Thanks very much.

ORWELL: I'm simply saying—

CARLOTTA: I understand what you're saying.

(This last CARLOTTA says angrily. Bitingly. ORWELL, in response, tries to temper himself, though he too can barely contain his emotion.)

ORWELL: We must control the message. I would rather…in this confusing environment…where the audience is coming into the discussion with a great deal of misinformation and prejudice…that we not *add* to it. Surely you must recognize the merit of such an argument.

CARLOTTA: Surely I do.

(This last CARLOTTA says drily—causing ORWELL to react in pique.)

ORWELL: *(Miffed)* I'm sorry. Have I offended you?

CARLOTTA: Why would you say that?

ORWELL: I have a sense in the superciliousness of your reply that I have.

CARLOTTA: Yes, well…perhaps you're right. And perhaps, as I think of it, I should act on that fact. *(Suddenly, she stands up.)*

ORWELL: *(Alarmed)* What are you doing?

CARLOTTA: What does it look like?
(She gathers her coat.)

ORWELL: I… *(Seeing she's putting it on)* …Oh, for God's sake, Carlotta!

(CARLOTTA spins around then, angrily.)

CARLOTTA: Let me ask you a question. Do you not find it at all *odd* that you would talk to me so?

ORWELL: How… What do you mean?

CARLOTTA: I mean given the subject matter, do you not find it at all odd?

ORWELL: I—

CARLOTTA: ...that in talking about Stalinism, you would expect me not to express my thoughts!

ORWELL: That is not...you've misunderstood.

CARLOTTA: I don't think so.
(She turns away again, going over to the coffee table, collecting her books.)

ORWELL: Carlotta, you have every right to express your thoughts. I am simply saying—

CARLOTTA: I know exactly what you're simply saying. And so does your audience, Mister Blair. *(Looking up)* All too well. All—

ORWELL: They—

(When again CARLOTTA rises, even more enraged!)

CARLOTTA: They understand, as I do, the precise nature of this exchange. It is not free!

ORWELL: Look—

CARLOTTA: Which begs the question—actually it raises an entirely *different* question...one that I've been meaning to ask you from the start. What exactly did you think you would *find* when you came here? Surely you've read our newspapers. You're aware of our climate. Alger Hiss. Richard Nixon. The Hollywood... whatever they're called... Surely you're aware of the moment we're in.

ORWELL: Yes, of course! That's—

CARLOTTA: And yet you're surprised, it seems— every *time*—when you get the reaction you do. When people who love your book, who think of you as their champion, who expect you to stand up with them against Communism, *wail* at you that you are betraying them!

ORWELL: But that's the point. I am not—

CARLOTTA: I understand your point. I understand your point precisely. What I *don't* understand, what our audience does not understand, is how you expect to make it! *(Beat)* I mean, for God's sake, why are you so impatient with them, Mister Blair?!? What exactly do you *expect*???

*(*ORWELL *stares at* CARLOTTA, *moved...frightened... inspired.)*

ORWELL: I... *(Giving up)* ...don't know.

CARLOTTA: Well, perhaps you should think about it. *(Again, she turns back.)*

ORWELL: Carlotta, please, don't go.

CARLOTTA: *(Beneath her breath)* I can't stay.

ORWELL: Why? What... *(Pleading)* Why?

CARLOTTA: *(Impatient, bitter)* Because you don't hear me, Mister Blair. When I speak, you don't hear. And I don't...I've done all I can.
(She starts for the door.)

ORWELL: I'll try.

CARLOTTA: Try?

ORWELL: And do... *(He is lost.)* ...what you're suggesting, what...

CARLOTTA: What am I suggesting?

ORWELL: You're...I think you're... *(Then, again, giving up)* I don't know.

(Beat. CARLOTTA *is seething with frustration, not knowing if she should continue. When she does, she stumbles, barely able to control her emotions.)*

CARLOTTA: Mister...Blair...Eric...do you understand what America is thinking at this point? And why we are thinking it?

ORWELL: I think so.

CARLOTTA: We are locked, do you see, *locked*...in a
struggle...we are caught, mightily, in an existential
struggle and we will not give up that struggle because
someone we admire *"tells—us—to"*. *(Slight beat)* And
so yes you can make your point...with humor...
with lightness...you can hope an audience, *part of an
audience,* thinks, ever so slightly...differently than they
did when you started... *(Becoming angry)* ...but you
cannot hope to "convert them"! And you cannot hope
they respond, in every instance, the way you *want them
to.* And when they respond differently, when they
express disappointment...incredulity...*anger*... *(Again
takes a moment, making sure he understands)* ...you must
anticipate that reaction...and respond with kindness.
Or I don't know what it is you hope to accomplish.

(Long pause. Again ORWELL *is moved, shaken even.)*

ORWELL: I think I want to impress you. I think—

CARLOTTA: It's not *about* me!

ORWELL: *(Heartsick)* It is. In part. *(Beat)* It is.

(Again CARLOTTA *turns away.)*

CARLOTTA: Well, I can't—

ORWELL: I want you, Carlotta. *(Adding, emotionally)* I...
want you.

(Only to turn back to ORWELL.*)*

CARLOTTA: You... *(Disgusted)* ...what???

ORWELL: I want you.

CARLOTTA: *(Beat, bitterly)* Well, I'm twenty-eight years
old. I have a boyfriend. I'm not available.

(This last CARLOTTA *snaps out—her rebuff brutal. Final.
Cold. Only to realize the moment she's said it—how crushed*
ORWELL *is by it.)*

ORWELL: I...

CARLOTTA: I'm sorry. *(Beat, repeating)* I'm sorry. *(Beat)* Look—

ALBANY VOICE: Ridiculous!

(Suddenly the lights return to the auditorium, ORWELL spinning around to face the speaker.)

ORWELL: What is?

(And instantly CARLOTTA is at ORWELL's side, once again his loyal lieutenant. Her coat is off again.)

ALBANY VOICE: That last part. About—

CARLOTTA: *(To ORWELL, whispering)* He's misunderstood.

ORWELL: You've misunderstood.

CARLOTTA: You're not saying you're not grateful.

ORWELL: Of course, I'm not. I'm—

ALBANY VOICE: *(Aggrieved)* Like it wasn't *hard for us.*

ORWELL: That is not what I'm saying! I... *(Impatient)* Look, I am not suggesting America did not sacrifice. You most certainly did. I am simply suggesting that in understanding *post*-war America, and *post*-war Europe, you keep in mind what has *occurred* over there. I mean, good God, there are entire countries over there that were entirely flattened, eliminated! *(Beat)* I was in Germany in the last months of 1945 and I cannot tell you what it looked like! *(He takes a moment to imply the thought—the devastation that he's seen. And how different it is from America.)* And so the people today, in the democracies we want them to *have*...are going to vote with a very different perspective from the one you have here. *(Beat)* That's all I'm saying.

ANOTHER ALBANY VOICE: *(Sympathetic)* They're going to vote socialist.

(This last is from a woman not unlike the woman from earlier, the one whom ORWELL *came to realize was an ally.)*

ORWELL: They're...yes. Some of them. Yes. *(Beat)* Absolutely. *(He looks at the audience member, the first Albany voice, trying to reassure him.)* That's all I'm saying.

(Then, after a moment)

CARLOTTA: Are you encouraged?

ORWELL: What?

CARLOTTA: Next question. *(Waving a card)* "Are you encouraged?"

ORWELL: Oh. *(Beat)* Oh yes. I am. I...put it his way, I think it's safe to be cautiously... *(Holding up a finger, warning)* ...we need to be careful now..."cautiously"... optimistic. However—

*(Suddenly, the lights change and we're once again in the hotel room—*CARLOTTA *and* ORWELL *facing each other, the tone once again quiet, measured—but, from him at least... extremely needy—and urgent. Though he takes a moment before talking.)*

ORWELL: Could I ask you something?

CARLOTTA: Yes.

ORWELL: Why— *(Then, thinking better of it)* No, never mind.

CARLOTTA: What?

ORWELL: I just feel...that time you sat near me. Why did you do that?
(His question has understated urgency to it—and grievance.)

CARLOTTA: What do you mean?

ORWELL: I mean, I asked you to sit near me—and you did.

CARLOTTA: Yes?

ORWELL: Why?

CARLOTTA: *(Beat)* Because you asked me to.

ORWELL: You didn't... *(Faltering)* ...there wasn't...

(A moment passes.)

CARLOTTA: What?

ORWELL: *(Needy)* It didn't *mean* anything?

(Another moment passes.)

CARLOTTA: It meant... *(Beat)* ...look, let's... *(Beat)* It just meant I wanted to be friendly.

ORWELL: Oh please! Don't... *(Softer)* Please, Carlotta.

(Long pause)

CARLOTTA: All right. *(Ashamed)* All right, you're right. It meant I wanted you to have hope.

ORWELL: That something might develop.

CARLOTTA: Yes.

ORWELL: Even though you knew it wouldn't.

CARLOTTA: Yes. *(Repeating, with more difficulty)* Yes.

(Another moment passes.)

ORWELL: Well, I can't be the first old man to be in this position.

(Long pause)

ORWELL: So—

CARLOTTA: I'm sorry. *(Long beat)* I'm sorry.

(Another pause)

(Then suddenly the lights change again—and again we're in the auditorium, CARLOTTA looking down at her question.)

CARLOTTA: Is... *(Stopping herself)* No, I shouldn't ask this, I...

ORWELL: What? *(Beat)* What does it say?

(CARLOTTA looks up at ORWELL, not wanting to continue.)

CARLOTTA: "Is your wife with you? *(Then, after a beat)* "Is your wife Eileen with you?"

(At this, ORWELL blanches.)

ORWELL: Oh. *(Beat)* No...she isn't. She...uh... *(Beat)* ... she died. In fact... She... *(Trying to be matter-of-fact)* She died. *(The pain hits him hard as he says this. Then, bravely, to audience)* But thank you for asking. *(There is a silence then. Which is uncomfortable for him.)* Actually, it was just after the war...when I was in Germany. When I was...reporting from there. Something to do with the lack of available medicines. The— *(Laughing, trying to make light of it)* You can't *imagine* the shortages. *(Beat)* In any case, the surgery itself was unremarkable. Or so I was told. And that's why I left, I...we had discussed it before I went off. Should I stay or should I go? And we both agreed I should go. *(Beat)* We had just adopted a boy. You see. I have a... *(His voice catching)* ...I have a three year old boy. *(Beat)* And I wouldn't have left if... *(Here he stops, momentarily overcome.)* But as I say... *(Again he stops.)* In any case, it led to a rather difficult year, last. A number of...what would you call 'em... embarrassing episodes? It seemed every girl I met I asked to marry. *(He nearly laughs, appalled by his own behavior.)* If you can believe it. As a mother for the child certainly...but...well, also I suppose I'd gotten used to the warm muffins and such. The... *(Beat)* And so, as I say, some embarrassing incidents. *(After a moment, brightening)* But all coming to an end I believe. Sad... sad days... *(Glancing over at CARLOTTA, wistfully...)* Sad days coming to an end. *(Before turning back to the audience)* But again, thank you for asking. I— *(To another part of the audience)* And please, if you know of a girl I should meet…please *do* leave a number, would you? I'd…

(This last ORWELL *says as a joke, which falls flat—creating a pall. And* CARLOTTA, *at least for a moment, doesn't know how to react. Then, after a beat, she looks down at her cards—and instantly he knows he's misstepped.)*

CARLOTTA: *(From the cards)* Do—

ORWELL: Actually…if… *(Beat, ashamed)* …I'm afraid I may have left the wrong impression—with that last. And I don't want to do that. *(Long beat, pained)* Eileen O'Shaunessy was the finest person I have ever known. *(Beat)* I loved her with all my heart. *(Long pause)* And I wouldn't want to leave any other impression than that. *(Again he is caught for a moment in the emotion. Then…)*

CARLOTTA: *(Quietly)* Children?

ORWELL: Hm?

CARLOTTA: Do—

ORWELL: Yes. I said. A boy. *(Beat)* I have…I have a three year old boy. *(Again, caught in emotion)* A lovely…a lovely boy. *(There is a silence—he, again, obviously moved.)*

RHINEBECK VOICE: *(Beat)* What's his name?

ORWELL: Richard. *(Beat)* Richard Blair. *(Brightening)* And we have a wonderful housekeeper who is doing just splendidly with him. Truly. Splendidly! *(Beat)* And is teaching me everything! *(Long beat)* So—

(Suddenly the lights come up on the hotel—and CARLOTTA *speaks immediately.)*

CARLOTTA: I'm sorry.

ORWELL: Don't—

CARLOTTA: I lied. Before. *(Beat)* About my boyfriend. *(Long beat)* I don't have one.

ORWELL: Ah.

(At this point there is an ease between CARLOTTA *and* ORWELL—*a quietness. No longer are they playing the sexual game; and that has relaxed them. Though she clearly wants to make amends.)*

CARLOTTA: I *had* one. *(Beat)* I... But he wanted a housewife.

ORWELL: And that's not you.

CARLOTTA: No.

*(*CARLOTTA *and* ORWELL *both laugh.)*

ORWELL: No.

CARLOTTA: Publishing—

ORWELL: Doesn't allow for it.

CARLOTTA: No. *(Laughing more)* It doesn't.

ORWELL: Long hours.

CARLOTTA: Extra credit.

ORWELL: *(More laughing)* Yes.

(Beat)

ORWELL: Well, don't trouble yourself. It's a lie...I'm sure I would have told as well. If I were in your place. *(Long beat)* Don't trouble yourself. *(Beat)* Not one bit.

(Beat)

CARLOTTA: Did...?

ORWELL: Hm?

CARLOTTA: No—different subject. Something I've been wondering. *(Proceeding cautiously, knowing she is on dangerous ground. Long pause)* Whether you had a chance to think about...what I said to you before. About...about why you say what you say...to our people. *(Beat)* Our audiences. *(Slight beat)* Why you're so impatient with them. *(Beat)* Why you don't...why you don't allow for discussion.

ORWELL: Ah. *(Long pause. He truly thinks about it.)* Well, I think perhaps you're right. Because of the moment we're in. *(Then)* And the guilt.

CARLOTTA: The guilt?

ORWELL: Yes...the... It's clear that what I've written is being used by people who don't share my opinion—about anything other than Stalin. And Communism. They don't share—

CARLOTTA: Could I stop you? For a second? I'm not talking about "those people". The publishers, the writers. The government. I'm talking about our audience. *(Beat)* The people in our audience. The people who *might* be open to you...and what you have to say...if you were more gentle with them. *(Beat)* And I wonder why you aren't.

(Long pause. And for the first time, ORWELL truly looks inside himself—and draws out the truth.)

ORWELL: Because I don't like them. I'm afraid. *(Beat)* I don't really like them.

CARLOTTA: *(Shocked)* Why not?

ORWELL: I don't know. Perhaps... *(Beat)* I don't know.

CARLOTTA: What were you going to say?

ORWELL: I've written about Eton. *(Long beat)* Where I went to school. How "rarified" an atmosphere, how "exclusive", how "undemocratic" ...and yet every friend I have today...*every* friend... *(Slight beat)* ...went to school in a similar place. Eton. Harrow. *(Holdings out his hand to her, an American)* Exeter. *(Beat)* It's all I know.

CARLOTTA: But it isn't. You know Spain as well. *The Road to Wigan Pier!* Paris. London. The places for the poor!

ORWELL: As a visitor. Always… *(Long pause)* …as a visitor. My home…is Eton. *(Pause)* It has always been Eton.

(Beat)

CARLOTTA: Well, we're not so bad you know. Those of us who didn't go to Eton. *(Long beat)* You should give us a chance.

(Beat. ORWELL *stares at* CARLOTTA.*)*

(Suddenly the lights change, and ORWELL *once again turns out, the audience in front of him. He is caught for a moment—taking his time before speaking.)*

ORWELL: I'm trying… *(Regrouping.)* …to think what should I leave you with…because tonight…tonight is our last… *(A brief pause, not able to finish the sentence.)* And perhaps it is this. We are locked…as many before me have said…we are locked…in a titanic struggle… against Communism. And in this struggle, this… "existential" battle…we will defeat *them*…or they will defeat *us*. And I hope, when we *do* defeat them—as I fully expect that we will—I hope that what emerges is a society that *cares for itself*. And each other. *(Loving)* And does not reward its soldiers…those from the very bottom who will fight, as they always do, all our battles…I hope we will not reward them with a new set of shackles. *(Beat)* That is my hope. *(Beat)* I hope you will share it with me. And that you will read my book…or *re*-read my book…*Animal Farm*…with that thought in mind. *(Beat)* That the battle against Communism is merely step one. Step two, an equally, perhaps even *more* necessary step…is Socialism. Democratic socialism. The Socialism, as its followers like to say…of the Rose. *(Pause)* So—

CARLOTTA: Oh! Everyone…make sure to sign up for… *(To* ORWELL*)* …what's it called?

(ORWELL *looks back at* CARLOTTA *not understanding—
shrugging.*)

CARLOTTA: Your new book.

ORWELL: Oh. Yes. *1984.*

CARLOTTA: *1984,* yes. *(To audience)* Please sign up for
Mister. Orwell's new book…*1984*… There's a list in
the lobby. *(Beat)* Thank you. *(And again she looks over at*
ORWELL.*)*

ORWELL: And from me as well. Thank you. And—

(And again CARLOTTA *and* ORWELL *are in the hotel, she
speaking immediately, excited.)*

CARLOTTA: They were transfixed. I'm telling you, at the
end there…transfixed.
(In her excitement, she hugs him.)
Really. You *had* them. *(Beat, meaningfully)* And you had
me as well.

ORWELL: *(Moved)* Did I?

CARLOTTA: You did, yes. And I'm telling you, if my
father were here to hear me say that. *(Beat)* You have
no idea what… *(She laughs.)*

ORWELL: *(Pleased)* Well, you answered my question
then.

CARLOTTA: What question?

ORWELL: I was going to ask…if anything I had said…
(Beat, trying to find another way to say it) …if I had
changed you at all. *(Continuing, needy)* And it seems,
just a little, I have.

(Pause. CARLOTTA *sees how much* ORWELL *needs it.)*

CARLOTTA: You have. *(Beat)* You really have.

(Long pause)

ORWELL: You know I was thinking about what you
said…to me…before. About the… About why I *do*

what I do. *(Beat)* Do you remember? Why... And I realized... I realized I was like a politician...in a sense. I... Right? Churchill. Atlee, Truman. Stalin even. Why do they do what they do? You know? Where does the impulse come from? Is it to do good? Or is it merely to leave an impression? And to the extent it's the latter, but they *do* make things better—and I know they often makes things worse, but to the extent they make things better—what do we think about that? Knowing that their motives were personal. That they had a *personal* need. Does it make what they do any less meaningful? *(Pause. Contemplating)* Well, I don't know. But I do know that it's true. At least for me. I know... And it isn't that I don't believe what I say. I do. But *why* I say it, why I *believe* it...why I believe it so *strongly*...that I think might be different from what I would have said two weeks ago. *(Long beat. Then, with great meaning)* I want to make an impression. I want to leave *you*...with an impression.

CARLOTTA: And you have. *(Beat)* You do.

(ORWELL *reaches out, touching her face.*)

ORWELL: Well. There's your answer then. *(Taking a moment—a trace wistful)* That's why I do what I do. *(Beat)* I want to leave an impression.

(ORWELL *turns out now, facing the audience, the lights fading, as he does, on* CARLOTTA.)

ORWELL: I want to leave everyone...everyone who knows me as George Orwell and not Eric Blair...with an impression. *(Beat)* I want you to think of me. I want you to *think* of me.

(*At this,* ORWELL *turns to the back wall where his writing suddenly appears.*)

ORWELL: I want you to think of me.

(And even as the lights go out on ORWELL, *they remain up on the words he has written, words that changed the 20th Century, words that even today remain among the most important, relevant, persuasive writings on the subject of politics ever written. Those words remain up for us to wonder at...)*

(And be moved by.)

(And then those words as well...fade to black.)

END OF PLAY

ADDENDUM

The play was originally performed with a cast of three characters: ORWELL, CARLOTTA, *and a* YOUNG MAN. *This last character appears only in act one and only briefly, and the version used in that first production is the one presented in this text. However, the author believes the play can be performed nearly as effectively without that third character, and what follows is the dialogue in ACT ONE as it would play between* ORWELL *and* CARLOTTA *making the play a two-hander. It begins in the middle of page 18.*

ORWELL: ...which in turn meant that I had to find another way of getting there. For I lost none of my purpose. None of my commitment. In fact, I had determined, and I now pledged myself yet again—that before I did anything else, before I wrote another *word* I would absolutely do my part in the struggle. *(Beat)* And so I made a fateful decision, (one that I question to this day) and used my "Independent Labour" contacts...to get to Barcelona. *(Slight beat)* Except for one slight problem. My new wife was insisting on coming with me. *(Beat)* Now gentlemen...

(When suddenly a stage door bell rings. It stops ORWELL.*)*

ORWELL: What the ...

(It rings again.)

ORWELL: Would someone…? *(Looking around)* What on earth…? Carlotta. *(Looking offstage, then)* Carlotta! *(Then, to audience)* Be… *(Holding up his hand)* Very sorry. *(Then)* Carlotta!

(At this, ORWELL starts to walk offstage, only to have CARLOTTA suddenly enter.)

CARLOTTA: Yes?

ORWELL: Are you not hearing this?

(The bell rings again.)

CARLOTTA: Oh. Yes.

ORWELL: Would you do something about that?

CARLOTTA: Yes, absolutely. *(To audience)* So sorry.

(With that, CARLOTTA walks off, leaving ORWELL awkwardly facing the crowd.)

ORWELL: Terribly sorry. I…I have no idea… Not… *(Only to be startled again)* Hey now, what's this?

(As CARLOTTA suddently emerges from the stage door area, now carrying a box of groceries.)

CARLOTTA: Your grocery delivery.

ORWELL: My…what??

CARLOTTA: Did you not have a grocery delivery?

ORWELL: Did…oh, my goodness. Yes. Yes, I did. *(To audience, excited)* My grocery delivery! *(Back to her)* My grocery delivery. Yes. Oh my goodness. *(He now goes over to her, taking the box of groceries.)* Did he bring… *(Looking inside)* Oh, yes, he did.

CARLOTTA: Very nice fellow.

ORWELL: *(Distracted)* What's that?

CARLOTTA: The young man. *(Looking back)* Strapping fellow.

ORWELL: Oh. Hmm. *(To audience, playfully)* Seems like someone might have a date after this.

(CARLOTTA blushes.)

CARLOTTA: In any case…if that's all?

ORWELL: Oh yes. Thank you so much. Carlotta… Carlotta Morrison. *(Then suddenly)* Oh, actually, wait, one minute. So long as I have you. I wonder if you could give me a hand here…with…

(Here ORWELL puts down the groceries, and after gesturing with this head, leaves with CARLOTTA, the two of them soon offstage and talking in hushed voices.)

ORWELL: *(Off stage)* Here, no embarrassment.

CARLOTTA: *(Off stage)* No.

ORWELL: *(Off stage)* You did splendidly.

CARLOTTA: *(Off stage)* Thank you.

ORWELL: *(Off stage)* If we could just bring the table.

CARLOTTA: *(Off stage)* What's that?

ORWELL: *(Off stage. With his head)* The table?

(And with that, CARLOTTA and ORWELL soon re-enter, now carrying a long folding table.)

ORWELL: That's it…

(ORWELL guides CARLOTTA.)

ORWELL: …and…just over here. Yes, indeed. Oh, thank you. Again, Carlotta Morrison everyone! *(To her then, genuine)* Thank you.

(CARLOTTA bashfully nods—and exits.)

ORWELL: Isn't she something? *(Watching her go, beaming)* Splendid. Splendid help. In any case… *(Only to look down again, once again pleased by his groceries.)* I'm sure you're wondering what I have here… *(Picking up the box.)* …and how it applies to you. *(He heads*

over with it to the table.) Well, it doesn't entirely. There
is… *(Setting it down—fishing around)* …for example…
(Pulling out a whiskey bottle) …my newfound fondness
for American whiskey. *(Then he flourishes playfully.)*
This is entirely…for me. *(At which point he unscrews the
bottle—and is about to take a drink…when he momentarily
pulls back.)* Well not entirely perhaps. I might, as the
evening progresses…invite a companion. *(Before
knocking back a jolt)* But still, off the point. The point at
the moment, this box, what's in it? And here I must
tell you, my pleasures of this last week. And my
impressions of America. *(Bursting out)* Good God!

VOICE: *(Hostile)* You prefer Russia???

The dialogue then resumes in the middle of page 22.

www.ingramcontent.com/pod-product-compliance
Lightning Source LLC
Chambersburg PA
CBHW052211090426
42741CB00010B/2499